What is Philosophy and Why Study It?

The Case for Relevance

Max Malikow

What is Philosophy and Why Study It?

Copyright © 2020 by Max Malikow

ISBN 9781733454025

Dedication

To Michael Schillace: Whose curiosity about truth and life's meaning marks him as a true philosopher - a lover of wisdom.

Preface

George Orwell said he wrote because he had to and not to have written would have gone against his nature. Similarly, the best reason for someone to study philosophy is that he must and not to study it would go against his nature. I study, teach, and write philosophy because I naturally think philosophically and long ago concluded not to do so would be incompatible with my disposition. Nevertheless, perhaps ironically, I've long maintained sympathy for students who do not share my intrinsic interest in the "love of wisdom" (*philein + sophos*).

This modest book is intended to encourage the study of philosophy by making a case for its practicality. Contrary to the widespread misperception that philosophy is irrelevant to real-life, philosophy not only can be practical, it must be practical if it is to be taken seriously as a subject worthy of study.

In *A Midsummer Night's Dream* Shakespeare describes the poet as one who imagines "the forms of things unknown" and "turns them to shapes and gives to airy nothing a local habitation and a name" (Act V, scene 1). Like Shakespeare's characterization of the poet, in this book I have tried to make the abstract and abstruse recognizable and understandable. Wanting to present my argument in the most accessible language possible I have written in the first person voice. In addition, in the interest of gender neutrality, I have used the alternating pronoun style.

Max Malikow,
Syracuse, New York
September 2, 2019

Table of Contents

*From The Best Things in Life by Peter Kreeft. Copyright ©
1984. Used by permission of InterVarsity Press,
www.ivpress.com.

Introduction: Why This Book?

I want to learn and I learn best by teaching, and writing is a form of teaching.

- Peter Kreeft

For me, locating the point at which a writing project began is an impossibility. Some of my experiences generate thoughts that percolate unawares until they surface as an idea for a book. Steve Jobs understood this dynamic and said, "You can't connect the dots looking forward; you can only connect them looking backwards" (2014). Looking back on 34 years of teaching philosophy and psychology I now realize something that had been developing for over three decades. Beneath the threshold of my awareness I was trying to understand why many students were skeptical of the relevance of philosophy while few of them questioned the usefulness of psychology.

It's not difficult to understand why students find psychology, the science of mind and behavior, engaging. After all, they are human beings studying why they think, act, and feel as they do. People do not have to be narcissistic to be curious about their inner life and conduct. In contrast to psychology students, many philosophy students are not inherently interested in the study of the essential nature of knowledge, reality, and existence. This difference between psychology and philosophy students exists in spite of many of the topics addressed in psychology are also taken up in philosophy, albeit differently.

When the philosopher and psychologist William James revealed the first psychology lecture he ever heard was the one he gave there was no psychology department at Harvard, where he taught, or any other university. Now, over 100 years later, the distinction between psychology and philosophy is so entrenched that the thought they are related is incomprehensible to many. This incomprehension should not exist since both disciplines are concerned with human behavior. Granted, the psychologist's interest is why people behave as they do and the philosopher's concern is how people ought to behave. But implicit in even the most meticulous study of the *why* of behavior is the question of *how* people ought to behave.

Given the above, the purpose of this book is to make the case for the study of philosophy being as relevant to real life as is the study of psychology. Since I have written for philosophy students I offer a caveat to anyone who has encountered this book apart from an academic assignment: *Unavoidably, writing for a specific audience reduces the value of a book for readers who are outside the intended audience.* Still, I hope anyone who invests in reading the pages that follow will be influenced to believe that philosophy is indeed relevant to the pursuit of a rich and meaningful life.

I. Is Philosophy Relevant to Real Life?

Experience has shown, and a true philosophy will always show, that a vast, perhaps the larger, portion of truth arises from the seemingly irrelevant.

- Edgar Allan Poe

Question: What do you call a dozen philosophers at the bottom of the ocean? Answer: A good start.

- Anonymous

"Philosophers Playing Soccer" is a satirical skit produced by Monty Python in which history's eminent philosophers pay no attention to the ball while walking around the playing field, each lost in his own thoughts (1972). Long before Monty Python, William James was concerned about the caricature of philosophers being so heavenly minded they are no earthly good. In a lecture given in 1907 James conceded philosophy "bakes no bread," thereby admitting to his colleagues the value of their work as philosophers will never be as obvious as the production of a baker (p. 1). For this reason, he added, the primary challenge to all philosophers is to communicate the relevance of their ideas to "real life." James also admitted to the immensity of this task since philosophers' incessant "quibbling and doubting" are often obnoxious to common people (p. 1).

If philosophy is not a history of arguments among philosophers then what is it and what is its mission? One way of looking at philosophy is to see it as a collection of ideas intended to widen our perspective and contribute to our autonomy. Rarely, if ever, does a narrow point-of-view provide a benefit. In *Paradise Lost* John Milton writes, "A mind is not changed by place or time. The mind is its own place, and in itself can make a heaven of hell, a hell of heaven" (1667, I.11.253-255). Allowing that Milton's expression is poetic, no power of the mind could have made a Nazi concentration camp heavenly. Nevertheless, psychiatrist and Holocaust survivor Viktor Frankl devoted an entire book to the power of the mind make the intolerable tolerable. In the preface of *Man's Search for Meaning* he explains his motivation for writing his memoir, a classic in the literature of psychiatry:

> I had wanted simply to convey to the reader by way of a concrete example that life holds a potential meaning under any conditions, even the most miserable of ones. And I thought if the point were demonstrated in a situation as extreme as a concentration camp, my book might gain a hearing (1992, p. xiv).

Contemporary philosopher and podcast sensation Sam Harris shows agreement with Milton and Frankl with his assessment that,

Almost all our suffering is the product of our thoughts. We spend nearly every moment of our lives lost in thought, and hostage to the character of those thoughts. You can break this spell, but it takes training just like it takes training to defend yourself against a physical assault (2019).

Engagement with philosophy, which can occur in the context of psychotherapy, can be a part of the training that breaks the spell produced by injurious thinking. Aaron T. Beck, a psychiatrist and the founder of cognitive behavioral therapy (CBT), believes depression and anxiety are often the result of negative thoughts that are illogical and unsupportable. He coined the term "cognitive triad" for the unwarranted beliefs many people have concerning themselves, the world, and the future. Drawing illogical conclusions and believing things that cannot stand up to scrutiny make life excessively arduous and exhausting. Beck does not posit all negative thoughts are groundless; only those that are baseless are challenged in CBT. Like Socrates, Beck believes an examined life is the best possible life.

People who hold unsupportable beliefs about themselves, the world, and the future tend to overtrust their feelings. Consequently, they often draw a conclusion based on emotion and then construct a rationale for the conclusion with which they started.

Irvin Yalom is another psychiatrist who recognizes the relationship between philosophy and psychotherapy. He maintains there are four philosophical issues that emerge in psychotherapy when it continues for a substantial period of time:

- the meaning of life
- free will and responsibility
- the experience of aloneness
- death

Like four currents beneath the surface of a river, these four issues are implicitly addressed by patients. When explicitly discussing their thoughts, feelings, and behaviors, they imply concern about the significance of their life, consequences of their choices, secrets about themselves, and limited amount of time they have to "get things right."

A thread running through much of philosophy is the idea that we can liberate ourselves from our circumstances even if we cannot escape them. The stoic philosopher Epictetus taught, "The essence of philosophy is that a man should so live that his happiness shall depend as little as possible on external things" (2019). This concept is foundational to *logotherapy*, the school of psychotherapy founded by Frankl. Also known as *existential therapy*, it focuses the patient on what can be done in the present to contribute to a more optimistic future. This requires directing the patient's attention to things within her control and away from things beyond it. One thing within the control of virtually everyone is his thought life. When Jean Jacques Rousseau wrote, "Man is born free, but everywhere he is in chains" he expressed his belief that governments repress freedom rather than secure it for their citizens (1968, p. 49). Nevertheless, even the most repressive state cannot deprive a man of his freedom to think. It was this freedom that enabled James Bond Stockdale, Robert Shumaker, Jeremiah Denton, and other prisoners of war to endure unspeakable hardship and retain their sanity. The mind is also capable of overcoming another type of imprisonment - captivity in the past. Augusten Burroughs insists, "You cannot be a prisoner of the past against your will. Because you can only live in the past in your mind" (2012, p. 107).

Discussions of freedom, including the freedom to think, should encompass responsibility. Thoughts lead to actions and if we are responsible for our actions we are also responsible for managing the thoughts that precede them. Thoughts at the conscious level are subject to our control because we can choose to redirect our thinking. As Martin Luther said, "You cannot keep birds from flying over your head but you can keep them from building a nest in your hair" (2019). Although preventing a thought from materializing as an action can be difficult it is no less a responsibility. The philosopher Arthur Schopenhauer agreed with Luther and taught we are free to do whatever we desire but we cannot choose what to desire. The novelist and existential philosopher Jean-Paul Sartre went so far as to characterize the weight of responsibility for our actions as part of our condemnation: "I say that man is condemned to be free. Condemned because he did not create himself, yet in other respects free; because once thrown into the world, he is responsible for everything he does" (1957, p. 23). Likewise, Frankl addresses the inescapable relationship between freedom and responsibility with a hypothetical: "I recommend that the Statue of Liberty on the East Coast be supplemented by a Statue of Responsibility on the West Coast" (1959, p. 156).

Irrefutably, ideas have consequences, which is to say beliefs influence feelings, behaviors, and relationships. Philosopher Kevin Browne defines philosophy as "the study of ideas and their power in our lives" (2011, p. 125). Among the subjects philosophy addresses are knowledge, logic, ethics, the meaning of life, decision-making, pleasure, government, religion, justice, and death. Learning how to think about these subjects is indeed relevant to real life. Concerning the mundane, Browne writes, "we are influenced each and everyday by a world of ideas. Studying them in an effort to understand them and their effect on us is a worthy and important pursuit" (p. 125).

Ludwig Wittgenstein had no tolerance for airy abstractions. A 20th century German philosopher, he reduced the work of a philosopher to a single pursuit when he famously stated the aim of philosophy is "to show the fly the way out of the fly-bottle" (2009, p. 110). Using the metaphor of a fly trapped in a fly-bottle, he characterized human beings as trapped by their inclination to see things in misleading ways. The way out of the fly-bottle is to fly downward rather than upward. But this is counterintuitive to the fly. Wittgenstein elaborated on his metaphor by referring to our penchant for acting according to our inclinations. The fly can escape only by acting contrary to its instinct. Freedom from many of life's problems requires ignoring our intuition and considering unfamiliar alternatives. Accordingly, Wittgenstein writes,

> If I am puzzled philosophically, I immediately darken all that which seems to me light, and try frantically to think of something entirely different. The point is, you can't get out as long as you are fascinated. The only thing to do is to go to an example where nothing fascinates me (Klagge, 2016, p. 82).

An implication of this metaphor is just as getting out of the fly-bottle is the most important thing to the fly so also philosophy should provide a useful service by addressing the issues that are most important to us.

As stated in the introduction, the "relevance question" plagues philosophy professors more than any other academic. (If this is an overstatement it's a slight one.) Although a strong case can be made for the study of philosophy as pertinent to everyday life, the relevance of studying philosophy for any given individual cannot be determined until most of her life has been lived. (Aristotle made the same observation concerning a good life. He taught the determination that a life is good cannot be made until nearly all of that life has been lived.) A subject that seemed irrelevant to a 20 year-old student could prove to be invaluable by the time he is 50 years-old. For example, the study of logic, one of philosophy's six subcategories, is indispensable to the practice of criminal law. The celebrated attorney Gerry Spence makes this point in his bestseller, *How to Argue and Win Every Time* (1996). Noteworthy is this book's subtitle: *At Home, At Work, In Court, Everywhere, Every Day*. Any 20 year-old who has determined philosophy (or any other subject) will never be useful to her has presumed to know what her life will include over the next 30 or 40 years. As Browne points out, "none of us knows for sure what will happen next in our lives and so we can never be absolutely sure that a subject, any subject, will not be relevant" (2019).

Unfortunately, the manner in which some philosophers write discourages students from reading philosophy. A principle of writing too often ignored by philosophers is *writers should work diligently writing so their readers will not have to work diligently reading*. Martin Heidegger is a noteworthy philosopher who seems to have disregarded this principle. Concerning *existence* he writes: "(Existence) designates a mode of Being; specifically, the Being of those beings who stand open for the openness of Being in which they stand, standing it" (1956, p. 214).

Did you enjoy reading Heidegger's words? Did you find his thought easy to understand? Has your life been enriched by his analysis of existence? Likely you answered "no" to each of these questions. It is unlikely that most people would enjoy reading hundreds of pages and listening to hours of lectures consisting of expressions like Heidegger's.

The relevancy question must be taken seriously by those of us who teach and write philosophy. I submit philosophy is not merely an intellectual exercise that cannot be applied to real life situations. An experience that contributed to this conviction occurred several years ago when teaching an introductory philosophy course. The college bookstore informed me the day before the first class that the required textbook would not arrive for at least two weeks. Since it was a summer school class that would last only five weeks a two week delay was nonviable. I cancelled the book order and assigned the students to read the news section of two newspapers each day before coming to class. In addition, they were told to highlight any news story that stood out to them and/or seemed to concern a philosophical issue. Not only did the students faithfully do the reading but they enthusiastically participated in the classroom discussions. Moreover, the stories provided examples of every philosophical topic I had planned on addressing in the course. The word *ubiquitous* is an adjective meaning "found everywhere." The diversity of the news stories and the ease with which the students found stories with a philosophical component reinforced my belief that philosophy is not only relevant but also ubiquitous.

A similar experience occurred several years later when teaching another introductory course. A week or two into the course it was apparent that few of the students were reading from the assigned textbook. (It was a 400 page standard text consisting of essays written by renowned philosophers.) When I asked the students why they were not doing the reading they responded that it was too difficult to understand. Since the assignments were not being read I discontinued them and replaced them with news stories, essays, poems, letters, and excerpts from books I had accumulated from teaching other courses. Movie excerpts were also assigned. The ensuing in-class discussions showed the students were doing the alternative assignments. Encouraged by the discussions, I had the readings published as an anthology titled *Philosophy Reader: Essays and Articles for Thought and Discussion* (Malikow, 2011).

The Inevitability of Philosophy

Lest you be inclined to believe that philosophy has no practical applications, consider each of the following examples presented by Mark B. Woodhouse (*Preface to Philosophy*, 1980, pp. 25-26).

1. A neurophysiologist, while establishing correlations between certain brain functions and the feeling of pain, begins to wonder whether the "mind" is distinct from the brain?

2. A behavioral psychologist, having increasing success in predicting human behavior, questions whether any human actions can be called "free."

3. Supreme Court justices, when framing a rule to distinguish obscene and non-obscene art works, are drawn into questions about the nature and function of art.

4. A theologian, in a losing battle with science over literal descriptions of the universe (or "reality"), is forced to redefine the whole purpose and scope of traditional theology.

5. An anthropologist, noting that all societies have some conception of a moral code, begins to wonder just what distinguishes a moral from a non-moral point of view.

6. A perennial skeptic, accustomed to demanding and not receiving absolute proof for every point of view encountered, declares that it is impossible to know anything.

7. An IRS director, in determining which (religious) organizations should be exempt from tax, is forced to define what counts as a "religion" or "religious group."

II. What is Philosophy?

Humanity left childhood and entered the troubled but productive world when it started to criticize its own certainties and weigh the worthiness of its most secure beliefs.

- Daniel Robinson

Everything comes from something else and nothing is the cause of itself. The previous sentence is the kind of statement that provokes derision of philosophers, who often are seen as alternating between stating the obvious and speaking the incomprehensible. Classic philosophical questions include: Is it possible to know anything with absolute certainty? What is reality? What constitutes a good life and how is such a life attained? Is free will an illusion? Is the universe eternal or did a prior entity bring it into existence? Is morality absolute or relative to each culture? Does God exist? Is there an afterlife? And, of course, what is the meaning of life?

It is not unusual for a philosophy textbook or introductory lecture in a philosophy course to begin with the origin of the word *philosophy*. Although Socrates is sometimes credited with having introduced this term it is equally probable that Pythagoras coined it. (Neither produced a written record; Socrates' teaching was immortalized by Plato's writing and oral tradition preserved Pythagoras' ideas.) The word *philosophy* derives from the combination of two Greek words: *philein* and *sophia*. The former is one of four Greek words translated as "love" and means "the affection experienced in friendship." The latter is translated as "wisdom" and means "the quality of good judgment and common sense." Hence, a philosopher can be understood as *a friend of wisdom.*

The late Daniel Robinson, a distinguished scholar, offered this reflection on the nature of philosophy:

> But there is, nonetheless, a special feature of philosophy that really does mark it off from all (other perspectives). Not in the sense of being better, or more advanced, or reserved to a privileged few. The philosophical perspective is one of criticism, and, yes, skepticism. I hope this won't be taken as indelicate, or worse, heretical, but if God were to declare a truth to the community of philosophers, at least the best of them would say (and one would hope, worshipfully), "But how can we be sure of that?"
>
> What the scientist actually sees, through aided or unaided sight, what the poet dreams and the prophet has revealed to him, the philosopher must find through argument, analysis, doubt, and yes, disinterest. The operative word here is disinterest not *uninterest.* The blindfold that decorates the face of justice is intended to signify (that disinterest) would have the chips fall where they may. The verdict will depend on evidence, not on the rhetorical skill of the advocate (or) the wealth of the defendant.

This, needless to say, is the judicial ideal and, we know, it is rarely achieved. But it is the recognized ideal. So too in philosophy. Let the successful arguments fall where they may. We are prepared to abandon one that was long favored and accept one that we find personally odious. Philosophy takes a systematic and critical perspective on all the assumptions and claims that we in the other compartments of human endeavor accept (2004).

Robinson eloquently distinguishes the philosopher's work from that of the scientist, poet, and prophet. The scientist works from research; the poet from imagination; and the prophet from revelation. Robinson posits the philosopher earns truth "the hard way - by working for it" (2004). Reflection is the hard work of a philosopher. This hard work sometimes involves challenging fundamental assumptions taken for granted by people in other fields of study. An example of a largely unchallenged assumption is inscribed on the gravestone of Karl Marx. An excerpt from his writing, it reads: "The philosophers have only interpreted the world in various ways. The point, however, is to change it" (1998, p. 177). Although appealing, Marx's assertion raises at least two questions: *Why* should the world change? and, *What* change or changes would constitute improvement? Marx's utopia of a classless society in which its members would contribute according to their ability and receive according to their need is but one thought in the marketplace of ideas. Why should

Marx's view be preferred over that of Andrew Carnegie, who favored a benevolent capitalism? Carnegie professed a man of wealth should be "the mere agent and trustee for his poorer brethren ... doing for them better than they would or could do for themselves" (1889). He proposed that a man should spend the first third of his life acquiring an education; the next third accumulating wealth; and the final third dispersing it to worthy causes. (He lived out his proposal by distributing $350 million dollars to various charities and projects over the last 18 years of his life.) And the views of Marx and Carnegie differ from that of Ayn Rand, an objectivist philosopher who insisted an individual's noblest activity is productive achievement. She disdained all forms of charity, especially altruism. In *The Virtue of Selfishness* she writes:

> Altruism declares that any action taken for the benefit of others is good, and any action taken for one's own benefit is evil. Thus the beneficiary of an action is the only criteria of a moral value - and so long as that beneficiary is anybody other than oneself, anything goes (1961, p. viii).

Rand's contempt for altruism was driven by her belief that altruism is a form of suicide since altruists sacrifice their life to serve the interests of others. She maintained *selfishness* is a largely misunderstood word because it means nothing more than "concern with one's own interests" and its definition has no moral component.

Another frequently unchallenged assumption is heard from politicians who insist "everyone should pay her fair share of taxes" without elaborating on how a "fair share" would be determined and justified. Further, how could any formula proposed for determining a "fair share" be demonstrated as itself being fair?

The philosopher is the child who unflinchingly declares the emperor isn't wearing any clothes when everyone else is going along to get along. The philosopher is Detective Columbo who always has one more question in his search for truth. Paul Tillich captured the spirit and mission of philosophy when he said, "philosophical shock is the beginning of wisdom" (Weaver, 1948, p. xii).

Philosophy and the Questions It Seeks to Answer

The 18th century German philosopher Immanuel Kant encapsulated the study of philosophy as the attempt to answer four questions:

- What can we know?
- What can we hope for?
- How should we behave?
- What is a human being?

Albert Camus, like Sartre, a novelist and existential philosopher, is more expeditious than Kant, reducing the interest of philosophy to a single inquiry: "There is but one truly serious philosophical problem, and that is suicide. Judging whether life is or is not worth living amounts to answering the fundamental question of philosophy" (1955, p. 3). Camus is not encouraging anyone to commit suicide. Rather, he is making the point that anyone who chooses to live is declaring that her life is worth living. This being the case, it is her responsibility to construct a life for herself that is personally meaningful.

Philosophy's Subcategories

While not everyone engages in a formal study of philosophy, everyone practices it. The six subcategories typically covered in introductory textbooks and courses demonstrate people are frequently engaged in philosophical activity without realizing it. Even *metaphysics*, the most abstract and abstruse subcategory, is often discussed unknowingly. Briefly, the six subcategories are:

1. **Epistemology** is the theory of knowledge. It addresses the question, *When something is claimed as true, how is this claim verified?* If this seems a frivolous topic, imagine yourself as the defendant in a criminal trial.

2. **Logic** is the study of the principles of correct reasoning. It pursues the question, *Is a conclusion the product of a rational process?* If this seems an unimportant question, think

of a time in an argument when you were caught (or caught someone) in a contradiction.

3. **Ethics** is concerned with virtue. It is concerned with the question, *Is a thought, action or condition moral or immoral?* If this seems irrelevant to real life then you've never wrestled with the possibility of telling a lie or struggled with some other moral dilemma.

4. **Axiology** (also known as value theory) examines the task of assigning worth. It responds to the question, *What makes one thing more valuable than another?* If this seems inconsequential, recall a time when you had to decide how much you were willing to pay for something or another time when you had to consider sacrificing one thing in order to possess another.

5. **Aesthetics** is the study of sensual pleasure. It takes up the question, *What makes an object or experience pleasing or displeasing to see, hear, taste, touch or smell?* If this seems insignificant, consider why you prefer certain movies, books, music, and foods. Also consider why you enjoy the company of some people and avoid spending time with others.

6. **Metaphysics** is the study of ultimate reality. Science describes the material realm and how it operates. But there are curiosities beyond the reach of science. Science can describe the process of bodily decomposition, but it cannot provide an

answer to the question of whether an afterlife follows death. Metaphysics systematically ponders the question, *Is reality limited to the material realm or are there nonphysical realities that are imperceptible to the five senses and, therefore, inaccessible by scientific investigation?* If this seems trivial then you've never wondered at a funeral if the decedent has moved on to another form of existence.

III. Philosophy's Ultimate Goal: A Life Well-Lived

The greatest discovery of my generation is that human beings can alter their lives by altering their attitudes of mind.

- William James

For Socrates philosophy did not mean removing oneself from the world to meditate upon it; it meant getting involved in life, and essentially and carefully examining every facet of existence.

- Thomas Ellis Katen

Concerning the aim of philosophy, theologian Luke Timothy Johnson writes,

> Classical Greek philosophers Socrates, Plato, and Aristotle are fine - if thinking is what you want. But the word philosophy means "love of wisdom," not "love of thinking." What about solid advice about how to be a good father or friend; or how to grow old gracefully; or know what true happiness is? Where can you find philosophy that tells you not how to think well, but how to live well? (2007, p. 40).

The implication of Professor Johnson's observation is wisdom, rather than intelligence, is required for a well-lived life. Intelligence and wisdom are not synonymous; the former is the ability to acquire and understand information and the latter is the quality of good judgment. Even an intelligent man can exercise poor judgment in managing his life.

As is often the case in philosophy one question leads to another question. If the purpose of philosophy is the acquisition of wisdom in order to live well this raises the question, "What does it mean to live well?"

What constitutes a good life?

Aristotle offered a formula for a good life with the definition, "Happiness proves to be activity of the soul in accord with virtue" (1999, 109a.15). He believed a good life (Greek: *eudaimonia*) derived from personally meaningful activity and adherence to a moral code over a lifetime. According to him a good life requires making wise choices, some of which may be difficult because of frequent temptations to settle for easier tasks and immediate gratification. Adding to this difficulty is the paradox that good character is required to resist these temptations but it is only by resisting them that good character is built.

Eric Hoffer, a 20th century social philosopher, makes an intriguing assertion about happiness in his memoir, *Truth Imagined*:

> It is the testimony of the ages that there is little happiness - least of all when we get what we want.

Many outstanding persons who reviewed their lives in old age found that all their happy moments did not add up to a full day (1983, p. 94).

When Socrates said, "The unexamined life is not worth living" he meant the best possible life is a life in which a man understands why he thinks, feels, and acts as he does (Plato, 1914, 38a.5-6). The method of teaching that bears his name consists of a cooperative dialogue in which questions and answers stimulate critical thinking and test presuppositions. Socrates believed, "I cannot teach anyone anything; I can only make them think" (2019). The Socratic Method is much like psychotherapy when a therapist challenges a patient with questions intended to clarify beliefs and enhance self-understanding. Two questions the renowned psychiatrist Irvin Yalom uses with his patients are *What do you really want?* and, *Is your current lifestyle moving you closer to or farther from what you really want?* If a patient's answers reveal inconsistency then her work in therapy is to bring them into harmony. It will be suggested to her that either she really doesn't want what she claims or she'll have to alter her lifestyle to accommodate to her stated desire.

Epicurus, a 4th century BCE Greek philosopher, taught, "It is impossible to live the pleasant life without living sensibly, nobly, and justly, and it is impossible to live sensibly, nobly, and justly without living pleasantly" (2015). For Epicurus a pleasant life is not necessarily a life of ease devoid of pain and suffering. Rather, it is a life pleasing to the one living it which requires a life that is consistent with that individual's moral code. Aristotle also included adherence to a moral code as necessary for a good life. He taught a happy man is one "who lives in accordance with complete virtue and is sufficiently equipped with external goods, not for some chance period but throughout a complete life" (2009, 1101a10).

A failure to live consistently with one's own moral code is exemplified by Reverend Dimmesdale, a character in Nathaniel Hawthorne's classic novel, *The Scarlet Letter.* Set in Puritan New England, it is the story of a woman, Hester Prynne, whose extramarital affair resulted in an illegitimate child and the public scorn that accompanied adultery. Taking responsibility for her sin, Hester carries herself with dignity, raising her child and never disclosing the identity of her lover. Her lover, Reverend Dimmesdale, is the community's respected spiritual leader. The minister lives out his years maintaining his image as a man of God. However, his inauthentic life, known only to him and Hester, is powerfully described by Hawthorne:

> It is the unspeakable misery of a life so false as his, that it steals the pith and substance out of whatever realities there are around us, and which were meant by Heaven to be the spirit's joy and nutriment. To the untrue man, the whole universe is false – it is impalpable – it shrinks to nothing within his grasp. And he himself, in so far as he shows himself in a false

light, becomes a shadow, or, indeed, ceases to exist (1978, p. 107).

Another literary classic, Robert Waller's *The Bridges of Madison County*, tells the story of Francesca Johnson and Robert Kincaid. Set in the late summer of 1965, Kincaid stops at an Iowa farm house to ask directions. There he encounters Francesca Johnson, alone at home while her husband and two children are visiting the Illinois State Fair. He is a 52 year-old photographer on assignment for *National Geographic* seeking the location of seven covered bridges for a photo shoot. As he approaches the middle-aged woman on the front porch he sees, "She was lovely, or had been at one time, or could be again" (Waller, 1992, p. 16). This encounter begins a four-day romance, "an erotic, bittersweet tale of lingering memories and forsaken possibilities" (*Publishers Weekly*, 2006, p.2).

Waller makes no attempt through his characters to justify their adultery. His elegant prose describes and explains their passion without excusing their behavior. On the eve of the return of Francesca's husband and children, she refuses Kincaid's offer to run away with him while admitting to her lackluster life:

> Yes, it's boring in a way. My life, that is. It lacks romance, eroticism, dancing in the kitchen candlelight, and the wonderful feel of a man who knows how to love a woman. Most of all, it lacks you. But there's

this damn sense of responsibility I have. To Richard, to the children. Just my leaving, taking away my physical presence, would be hard enough for Richard. That alone might destroy him. As much as I want you and want to be with you and part of you, I can't tear myself away from the realness of my responsibilities (Waller, pp. 115-116).

Had she left with Kincaid she would have taken the weight of her responsibilities with her. She explains to him, "If I did leave now, those thoughts would turn me into something other than the woman you have come to love" (p. 116). He understood her decision, "He knew what she was saying about the road and responsibilities and how the guilt could transform her. He knew she was right, in a way" (p. 116).

If Kincaid knew Francesca's decision was right *in a way* does this imply that *in a way* her decision was wrong? "How should we behave?" is the fundamental question of ethical philosophy. Often, it is no easy task to determine our obligations. The seventh of the Ten Commandments is, "Thou shalt not commit adultery." Yet, nowhere in *The Bridges of Madison County* is adultery referred to as a sin. Francesca's decision to remain with her family was not religiously motivated. Instead, she explains her decision in terms of her responsibility to her family. After weighing her desire against her duty the scale tipped in favor of duty and she remained an Iowa farmer's wife. What accounts for her duty prevailing over her desire?

The list of philosophers who have pondered the question of moral conduct includes Thomas Hobbes, Immanuel Kant, Soren Kierkegaard, John Stuart Mill, and Friedrich Nietzsche. Some from this list argue that right and wrong are determined by the results produced by an action. They would insist if Kincaid and Francesca's adultery did not harm anyone then it was not morally wrong. Others from this list would maintain adultery is morally wrong even when it produces no harm because adultery is a forbidden act. Of course, this raises the question, "What makes an act forbidden?" If the answer is that it violates one of the Ten Commandments ("Thou shalt not commit adultery"), does this mean people who have no belief in God are nonetheless obligated to obey the Decalogue?

Concerning a good life, Mill makes a debatable claim when he writes,

> It is better to be a human being dissatisfied than a pig satisfied; better to be Socrates dissatisfied than a fool satisfied. And if the fool, or the pig, are of a different opinion, it is because they only know their side of the question. The other party to the comparison knows both sides" (2001, p. 10).

Mill was convinced an educated person would not choose ignorance over knowledge even if knowledge causes dissatisfaction. This is contrary to the well-known aphorism "ignorance is bliss." Ironically, this phrase is part of a line in a poem that says precisely the opposite and agrees with Mill's assertion. The complete line is, "Where ignorance is bliss, 'Tis folly to be wise" (Gray, 1886, p. 10).

Few people are as qualified as the aforementioned Daniel Robinson to speak about the characteristics of a good life. Widely recognized as a scholar in both psychology and philosophy, he believed, "The good life is active, contemplative, somewhat fatalistic, and selfless" (2004, Part 5, p. 8). He summarized a good life as one that is characterized by participation, reflection, some resignation, and charity.

The question of what constitutes a good life generates several other questions, among them: Can a delusional life be a good life? Does a good life require longevity? Is it possible for a life to be wasted? And, of course, what is the meaning of life? Each of these questions is addressed in the remainder of this chapter.

Can a delusional life be a good life?

Epistemology addresses the certainty of knowledge by asking, "When something is claimed as true, how can we be certain that it is?" Metaphysics addresses the scope of reality by asking, "Is reality limited to the physical realm or are there nonphysical realities?" Both subcategories converge on the question of whether a good life can be delusional. A well-known case study of a belief contradicted by reality was conducted in a Michigan psychiatric hospital by Dr. Milton Rokeach when he observed three patients, each of whom believed himself to be Jesus Christ. Rokeach placed them together in group therapy and other situations in the hospital. After two years of interacting with each other all three maintained his identity as the Son of God. Rokeach describes this fascinating case study in *The Three Christs of Ypsilanti* (1964).

Delusions are the defining feature of a *delusional disorder*, a type of psychosis in which people fail to distinguish what is real from what is imagined causing them to maintain a belief system that is incompatible with reality. This condition raises two philosophical questions: "How is reality determined?" and, "Is contact with reality necessary for a good life?" In the case of the three Christs, a third question is whether it was professionally ethical and morally right for Dr. Rokeach to attempt to dispel the men of their delusion. Years after the study Rokeach expressed regret for the attempt, saying he had no right in the name of science to interfere with their lives. In more ordinary situations, is it morally right to correct someone's belief, especially if it's inconsequential or if the correction will diminish her happiness? Might it be that a good life can include at least a little bit of delusion?

Is longevity necessary for a good life?

In a speech given the day before his assassination the Reverend Dr. Martin Luther King, Jr. said, "Like anybody, I would like to live a long life - longevity has its place" (1968).

Certainly, longevity can be part of a good life, but is it necessary for a good life?

Shakespeare's Macbeth described his life with these words: "Tomorrow and tomorrow and tomorrow creeps in this petty pace from day to day, to the last syllable of recorded time" (Act V. Scene 5). Solomon, the King of Israel, offered a similar reflection:

> All things are wearisome, more than one can say. What has been will be again, what has been done will be done again; there is nothing new under the sun. Is there anything of which one can say, "Look! This is something new"? (Ecclesiastes 1:8-10, NIV)

According to the biblical record, Solomon lived 60 years at a time when life expectancy at birth was 30 years and 50 years if a person reached the age of 20, (Frier, 2009, pp. 788-789). Yet he bemoaned the tedium of life in spite of immeasurable wealth which he did not spare in his pursuit of pleasure. If Solomon were the only one whose great wealth did not provide happiness then he could be seen as an anomaly. However, this is not the case. Lottery winners report they are no happier after winning millions of dollars than they were before (Brickman, Coates, and Janoff-Bulman, 1978).

Quaker philosopher David Elton Trueblood writes:

> Each of us is bound to die, and every rational person is highly conscious that his life is short, but there need be

no tragedy in this. It is surely not so bad to die, providing one has really lived before he dies. Life need not be long to be good, for indeed it cannot be long. The tragedy is not that all die, but that so many fail to really live (1951, p. 164).

Trueblood's observation concerning longevity is shared by Stephen Vincent Benet: "Life is not lost by dying! Life is lost moment by moment, day by dragging day, in all the thousand, small, uncaring ways" (1942). If Trueblood and Binet are correct, then *how* a man lives has more influence on the quality of his life than *how long* he lives. A life in which birth and death are separated by many years will not be appreciably different from a shorter version of that same life. A centenarian's life essentially would be a fourfold extension of that same life lived over 25 years. People who lack self-discipline would never get around to reading the classics or learning to play the piano regardless of how many years they have to accomplish these things. Since personality exerts the greatest influence on how a life is lived, some people could live blissfully for 100 years; others would multiply their misery; many would live nondescript lives; and still others would obsess interminably over what to do with so much time.

Is it possible for a life to be wasted?

The movie "Good Will Hunting" is the story of an off-the-charts genius who spurns a formal education and profession in favor of working as a construction laborer and carousing with his rowdy friends. When confronted about "wasting his life" he defends his lifestyle. He doesn't deny that he is a genius but argues that his intellect does not require him to live a life utilizing it.

A person can be said to be wasting his life when he is not doing what he is supposed to be doing. But who determines what an individual ought to be doing with his life and how is this determination made? Moreover, the assumption that there is an intended purpose for anyone's life is disputable. A fundamental teaching of nihilism is there is no purpose to anyone's life. Existentialism, the philosophical approach that emphasizes each individual is responsible for what she does with her life, maintains one person has no standing to tell another how her life ought to be lived. Of course, this leads to the question of the meaning of life.

What is the meaning of life?

Albert Camus writes, "You will never live if you are looking for the meaning of life" (2019). Philosopher Jay Garfield disagrees and writes:

> *What is the meaning of life?* It's a question every thoughtful person has pondered at one time or another. Indeed, it may be the biggest question of all. It is at once a profound and abstract question, and a deeply personal one. We want to understand the world in

which we live, but we also want to understand how to make our lives as meaningful as possible; to know not only *why* we're living, but that we're doing it with intention, purpose, and ethical commitment (2013, p. 1).

Why does the question of life's meaning persist in spite of 25 centuries of philosophy having failed at definitively answering it? Perhaps it is the intrinsic curiosity in virtually all human beings that drives them to ask for themselves, "What is the meaning of my life?" Frankl so strongly believed life is primarily a search for meaning that he disagreed with Freud, who insisted life is a pursuit of pleasure, and Alfred Adler, who taught life is a quest for power.

The significance or importance of an individual's existence is either constructed or discovered. If the meaning of life is constructed then it will be determined by the life a person creates for himself by his actions. If the meaning of life is discovered then some being or entity designed and produced a life for an intended purpose. If this is the case then it is the individual's responsibility to discover her assignment and fulfill it. This implies a Creator as described in the New Testament: "For we are God's workmanship, created in Christ Jesus to do good works, which God prepared in advance for us to do" (Ephesians 2:10, NIV).

In his analysis of the human condition the eminent psychiatrist Carl Jung concluded a failure to find a meaningful life accounts for the anxiety with which many people live:

Among my patients from many countries, all of them educated persons, there is a considerable number who came to see me, not because they were suffering from a neurosis, but because they could find no meaning in life or were torturing themselves with questions which neither present day philosophy nor religion could answer. Some of them perhaps thought that I knew of a magic formula, but I was soon forced to tell them that I, too, had no answer to give. It must be a relief to every serious-minded person to hear that the psychotherapist also does not know what to say. Such a confession is often the beginning of the patient's confidence in him (1933, p. 231).

IV. The Value of Thought Experiments

If what happened on your inside happened on your outside, would you still smoke?

- American Cancer Society Advertisement

Psychologist William Kirk Kilpatrick discourages the use of moral dilemmas in teaching ethics. He insists the moral quandaries seized upon by professors are too rare to be of value in teaching ethics. For example, it is true that some survivors of the ill-fated Titanic were in overcrowded lifeboats and the decision had to be made who would remain in the boats and who would be set adrift in the frigid North Atlantic and certain death. But Kilpatrick raises the question of the probability of any student ever being confronted with such a decision.

Like a roller-coaster ride, the dilemma approach can leave passengers a bit breathless. That is one of its attractions. But like a roller-coaster ride, it may also leave them a bit disoriented - or more than a bit. That, as a growing number of critics are suggesting, is one of its drawbacks.

The question to ask about this admittedly stimulating approach is this: Do we want to concentrate on quandaries or on everyday morality?

> The danger in focusing on problematic dilemmas is
> that a student may begin to think that all of morality is
> similarly problematic (1992, pp. 84-85).

If exceedingly rare situations are of dubious value for teaching moral philosophy it is reasonable to ask if impossible situations have a rightful place in teaching philosophy in general. Traditionally, philosophers have employed situations known as *thought experiments* to raise questions, clarify issues or advance arguments. The quotation introducing this chapter is a thought experiment in the form of a "what if" question from the American Cancer Society. In this chapter ten thought experiments are presented along with the rationale for their usage. As you read, consider their appropriateness for teaching moral philosophy.

The Ship of Theseus

The war ship of a legendary king named Theseus was retired and displayed as a memorial in his honor. As time went on the rotted planks of the ship were replaced. If all the planks are replaced is this ship still the ship of Theseus? If not, at what point did the ship cease to be the ship of Theseus? Was it when over 50 percent of the planks had been replaced? If it remains the ship of Theseus in spite of every plank of the ship having been replaced, how can this be since no part of this structure ever went to battle?

This thought experiment, presented by Plutarch, is applied to the question of personal identity. What makes any of us the same person over our lifetime? Given changes in our values, priorities, worldview, and physical structure how can it be said we are the same person in adulthood who we were in childhood?

Zeno's Paradox

"You can't get there from here" is an expression associated with the people of Maine when asked for directions. Zeno of Elea argued since the distance between two points can be reduced infinitely by one-half then it is impossible to reach a destination if the travel requirement is to continuously advance one-half of the remaining distance. In other words, since the distance between two points can always be reduced by one-half and the traveller must always go one-half of the remaining distance then it would be impossible to complete the journey.

Zeno's paradox illustrates the distinction between mathematical reality and experiential reality. Theoretically, the never-ending journey postulated by Zeno is possible in spite of no one ever having made it. Moreover, if someone set out to make such a journey, why would he? The value of Zeno's paradox is it serves as an illustration of the logical argument *reductio ad absurdum*. Also referred to as *argumentum ad absurdum, reductio ad absurdum* (Latin: reduction to absurdity) is a form of argument used either to disprove a statement or demonstrate it leads to an impractical conclusion.

The Brain in a Vat

To what extent can we trust our experiences? Rene Descartes posited the only knowledge each of us can embrace with certainty is that of our own existence. The brain in a vat experiment asks you to imagine the possibility that you are actually nothing more than a brain connected to a computer program simulating outside world experiences. If this thought experiment has a ring of familiarity it might be because of "The Matrix," the movie in which the entire human race is unknowingly trapped inside a virtual reality. It might also be familiar if you've encountered Descartes' concept of a powerful evil demon who deceives Descartes by presenting him with an external world of illusion.

If you are a brain in a vat does it follow that you cannot question anything you're experiencing? Thomas Nagel's answer to this question implies the value of this thought experiment:

> If I accept the argument (that I am a brain in a vat), I must conclude that a brain in a vat can't think truly it is a brain in a vat, even though others can think this about it. What follows? Only that I cannot express my skepticism by saying, "Perhaps I am a brain in a vat." Instead, I must say "Perhaps I can't even think the truth

about what I am, because I lack the necessary concepts and my circumstances make it impossible for me to acquire them!" If this doesn't qualify as skepticism, I don't know what does" (1986, p. 73).

One value of the brain in a vat exercise is its establishment of the impossibility of eradicating skepticism. Nagel correctly argues that even in the most restrictive circumstance imaginable the ability to doubt is retained.

Another value of this thought experiment is the opportunity it provides to test the assertion that happiness is the ultimate motivation for human activity. Admittedly, it's tempting to believe all behavior is directed toward happiness and once happiness is attained the destination has been reached. But is this true? If existence as a brain in a vat included a feeling of unremitting happiness would this be preferred over an actual life in a body outside the vat having real experiences? If my students over the years are an indication of what most people would choose, it would be the real life.

Where Was Jesse James Killed?

The outlaw Jesse James was gunned down on April 3, 1882 by Robert Ford, a member of his gang. The killing took place in James' home at 1318 Lafayette Street in St. Joseph's, Missouri. In 1939 the house was relocated and moved again in 1977 to its current location, two blocks from its original site.

What if someone built a replica of James' house on the lot at 1318 Lafayette Street? Would it be accurate to claim it as the actual site of Jesse James' murder? Would this relegate the relocated house to lesser historical status? If a dispute over the rightful claimant of the owner of the place where Jesse James was killed ended up in court and you were the judge, how would you rule?

The value of considering the actual location of Jesse James' killing brings out the importance of wording. President Bill Clinton made this clear when he famously said, "It depends on what the meaning of the word 'is' is." The President, defending his denial of a sexual relationship with Monica Lewinsky, maintained he did not lie because he answered in the present tense. At the time he was asked about the relationship he was not involved with Ms. Lewinsky, so he spoke truthfully when he said he *is* not sexually involved with her.

In everyday parlance the precise meaning of words is not as important as in legal proceedings and contracts. Nevertheless, what words mean is important often enough to carefully consider their use.

What Mary Didn't Know

Frank Jackson created one of philosophy's best known thought experiments when he placed Mary, a brilliant scientist specializing in the neurophysiology of vision, in a room from which she investigates the world. This room and everything in it is either black or white and Mary has never been outside of this room. Even the television monitor she watches is black and white. From her study of the world she is able to explain in detail how different objects produce different wavelengths on a retina causing people to say "red" when looking at a tomato and "yellow" when looking at a dandelion.

When Mary, who knows everything about the science of color, is released from her room will she learn anything? Jackson maintains she will. In spite of her complete knowledge of the *physical* aspects of color she will learn the *experience* of color when she leaves the room. Jackson formulated his thought experiment to demonstrate the error of *physicalism*, the belief that the body and the mind are essentially the same thing. If physicalism were correct then Mary would learn nothing following her release from the black and white room. Jackson maintains the mind and the body are two completely different entities, existing independently of each other.

The implication of this thought experiment is someone who has complete physical knowledge about another conscious being would still lack knowledge about how it feels to have the experiences of that other being. "What Mary Didn't Know" demonstrates the limitation of empathy. A knowledgeable, empathic psychiatrist might understand why a patient feels a certain way but cannot experience the life of that patient. Like the psychiatrist, we can never completely understand and share the feelings of another person because we can never *be* that person. At best, we can use our experiences to empathize with someone, but we cannot leave our life and enter into someone else's. (Nagel made the same point in his essay, "What Is It Like to Be a Bat?" [1974, pp. 435-450]).

The Mechanical Sweetheart

What if you found the perfect lover? A lover who is physically attractive, sexually exciting, intellectually stimulating, and compatible with you in every way. Convinced you have found your partner for life you then learn that your lover is not a human being but a perfectly built android. Would this matter to you? If so, why? What human feature is lacking in the android. This thought experiment is the work of William James. It provides an opportunity to consider the long-running debate between *monism* and *dualism*. Monists maintain reality is of one substance: the physical. Dualists believe there are two dimensions to reality: the physical and the immaterial. This debate has obvious implications for whether there is an afterlife. If dualists are right then we might have a nonphysical component that lives on after our physical death.

A Life of 450 Years

"Opsigeria: A Blessing or a Curse" is an essay in which the benefits and disadvantages of a 450 year life are contemplated (Malikow, 2010, pp. 77-84). (*Opsigeria* is a fictitious disease in which the aging process advances seven times more slowly than normal.) Considering this impossible life raises the question, "If longevity is not necessary for a good life then what are the ingredients of a life well lived?"

Shooting a Man Whose Death Is Inevitable

Of course, death is inevitable for all of us. But in the following thought experiment the inevitability of death is immediate.

> *Intending to commit suicide, a man jumps from the roof of a 40 story apartment building. In his descent he passes by the window of an apartment on the 20th floor just as a man in the apartment accidentally discharges a loaded shotgun he was cleaning. The pellets from the shotgun shell strike the suicidal man in the chest, instantly killing him. Is the man in the apartment guilty of manslaughter? (A murder in which the accused neither planned nor intended the victim's death.)*

The improbability of this event would seem to relegate it to irrelevance. However, it does have value in discussing the legal term *proximate cause*. Proximate cause is an event that results in the injury or death of someone. In the above case the negligence of the man cleaning the shotgun caused the death of the man who wanted to die and was going to be dead a second or two after being shot. Nevertheless, the negligence of the man in the apartment was the proximate cause of the descending man's death. In civil and criminal cases when the negligent act is established as the cause of injury or death it is referred to as the proximate cause. In the above case, in spite of the inevitability of the suicidal man's death, it was the shotgun blast that killed him. Since there is no intervening event that accounts for his death, the man in the apartment is guilty of manslaughter. Proximate cause is integral to establishing responsibility in many real-life situations both in and outside of court rooms.

A similar thought experiment is one in which a contract killer is hired to break into the home of his intended victim and shoot him. The hitman enters the home, finds the man asleep in bed, and fires three shots into his chest. The police are able to solve the crime and the hired killer is arrested. However, the medical examiner's autopsy establishes the cause of death as a heart attack that occurred several hours before the hitman did his work. In this case the proximate cause is the heart attack. Hence, the hitman is not responsible for this death and is guilty of nothing more than breaking and entering. (Given the impossibility of killing a dead man the hitman will have to refund his fee.) This thought experiment provides an opportunity to discuss the difference between intent and result. Can we be guilty of something we intended or desired but did not cause?

The Cogito and Eternal Recurrence

As previously stated, the 17th century mathematician and philosopher Rene Descartes pondered the certainty of knowledge and imagined an evil demon who controlled his perceptions and distorted every one of them into an illusion. In such a condition, Descartes wondered if he could trust any of his perceptions as being true. He concluded the reality of his own existence was the only unassailable truth he could assert. Even if every thought he had was the product of demonic deception his own existence was the one thing of which he could be certain. Even if he doubted his own existence it was he who was doing the doubting. The Latin expression for Descartes' conclusion is *cogito ergo sum*, translated as, "I think, therefore, I am" (2019).

It could be argued Descartes' evil demon thought experiment is irrelevant to real life since few, if any of us, go about questioning our own existence. If Descartes' romp into the theoretical has no existential connection the same cannot be said about Friedrich Nietzsche's similar excursion. In *Thus Spake Zarathustra: A Book for All and None* (1976) Nietzsche speaks through an aged prophet, replete with wisdom. The sage presents one of Nietzsche's most important ideas: "eternal recurrence." Presented as a hypothetical question, it asks: What if you were to live the life you are now living again and again throughout eternity - would this change you?

What if some day or night, a demon were to steal after you into your loneliest loneliness and say to you: "This life as you now live it and have lived it, you will have to live once more and innumerable times more; and there will be nothing new in it, but every pain and every joy and every thought and sigh and everything unutterably small or great in your life will have to return to you, all in the same succession and sequence The eternal hourglass of existence is turned upside down again and again, and you with it, speck of dust!" Would you not throw yourself down and gnash your teeth and curse the demon who spoke thus? Or have you once experienced a tremendous moment when you would have answered him "You are a god and never have I heard anything more divine." If this thought gained possession of you, it would change you as you are or perhaps crush you (1976, p. 341).

The eminent psychiatrist Irvin Yalom's commentary on "eternal recurrence" clarifies the real life value of Nietzsche's hypothetical:

> If you engage in this experiment and find the thought painful or even unbearable, there is one obvious explanation: you do not believe you've lived your life well. I would proceed by posing such questions as, How have you not lived well? What regrets do you have about your life?
>
> My purpose is not to draw anyone into a sea of regret for the past but, ultimately, to turn his or her gaze toward the future and this potentially life-

changing question: *What can you do now in your life so that one year or five years from now, you won't look back and have similar dismay about the new regrets you've accumulated? In other words, can you find a way to live without continuing to accumulate regrets?* (2008, p. 101).

Conclusion

The thought experiments presented above have value because each provides an occasion for considering and discussing fundamental questions that constitute not only philosophy but real life. The *Ship of Theseus* addresses the permanence of identity in the context of change. *Zeno's paradox* demonstrates the impracticality of some theoretically correct ideas. Putnam's *stimulated brain in a vat* challenges the assumption that the experience of happiness is life's ultimate meaning. The location of the killing of Jesse James implies the importance of precision in the use of words. Jackson's "What Mary Didn't Know" demonstrates the difference between knowledge and experience as well as the limitation of empathy. James' *mechanical sweetheart* is useful for considering whether belief in an immaterial afterlife is rational. "Opsigeria: A Blessing or a Curse?" opposes the belief that longevity is integral to a good life. Shooting a man whose death is inevitable or a man already dead provides an occasion for determining responsibility. Descartes *evil demon* reminds us perception is not necessarily reality. And

Nietzsche's *eternal recurrence* prompts us to evaluate how we are managing life.

V. "On Education and E. T." (Dr. Peter Kreeft)

Whom do I call educated? First, those who manage well the circumstances they encounter day by day.

- Socrates

Thoughtfulness can mean either kind or contemplative. When Socrates said, "The unexamined life is not worth living," he meant the richest life available is a life lived thoughtfully. According to Socrates, contemplation of why we think, act, and feel as we do adds value to our lives.

In his witty and insightful book, The Best Things in Life, *philosopher Peter Kreeft places Socrates on a contemporary college campus, Desperate State University. There Socrates has a series of conversations with the students and professors he finds there. The first of these interactions is with Peter Pragma, a student who seems to be living an unexamined life.*

Socrates: Excuse me for bothering you, but what are you doing?

Peter: What kind of silly question is that? I'm reading a book. Or was, until you interrupted me. Can't you see that?

Socrates: Alas, I often fail to see what others see, and see things others cannot see.

Peter: I don't get it.

Socrates: I saw you holding the book, yes, but I did not see you reading it.

Peter: What in the world are you talking about?

Socrates: You are holding the book in your hands, aren't you?

Peter: Of course.

Socrates: And I can see your hands.

Peter: So?

Socrates: But do you read the book with your hands?

Peter: Of course not.

Socrates: With what, then?

Peter: With my eyes, of course.

Socrates: Oh, I don't think so.

Peter: I think you're crazy.

Socrates: Perhaps, but I speak the truth, and I think I can show you that. Tell me, can a corpse read?

Peter: No …

Socrates: But a corpse can have eyes, can't it?

Peter: Yes.

Socrates: Then it is not just the eyes that read.

Peter: Oh. The mind then. Are you satisfied now?

Socrates: No.

Peter: Somehow I thought you'd say that.

Socrates: I cannot see your mind, can I?

Peter: No.

Socrates: Then I cannot see you reading.

Peter: I guess you can't. But what a strange thing to say!

Socrates: Strange but true. Truth is often stranger than fiction, you know. Which do you prefer?

Peter: You know, you're stranger than fiction too, little man.

Socrates: That's because I'm true too.

Peter: Who are you, anyway?

Socrates: I am Socrates.

Peter: Sure you are. And I'm E.T.

Socrates: I'm pleased to meet you, E.T.

Peter: My name is Peter Pragma.

Socrates: Do you have two names?

Peter: What do you mean?

Socrates: You said your name was E.T.

Peter: And you said your name was Socrates.

Socrates: Because it is. I have this strange habit of saying what is.

Peter: What do you want from me?

Socrates: Would you let me pursue my silly question just a moment longer?

Peter: I thought you got your answer.

Socrates: Not to my real question. You see, when I asked you what you were doing, I really meant *why* are you doing it?

Peter: I'm studying for my exam tomorrow.

Socrates: And why are you doing *that*?

Peter: You know, you sound like a little child.

Socrates: Thank you.

Peter: I didn't mean it as a compliment.

Socrates: I don't care. Only answer the question, please.

Peter: I'm studying to pass my course, of course.

Socrates: And why do you want to do that?

Peter: Another silly question! Don't you ever grow up?

Socrates: Let me tell you a secret, Peter: There *are* no grown-ups. But you still haven't answered my "silly question."

Peter: To get a degree, of course.

Socrates: You mean all the time and effort and money you put into your education here at Desperate State is to purchase that little piece of paper?

Peter: That's the way it is.

Socrates: I think you may be able to guess what the next question is going to be.

Peter: I'm catching on. I think it's an infection.

Socrates: What is the next question, then?

Peter: You're going to ask me why I want a degree.

Socrates: And you're going to answer.

Peter: But it's another silly question. Everyone knows what a degree is for.

Socrates: But I am not "everyone." So would you please tell me?

Peter: A college degree is the entrance ticket to a good job. Do you know how difficult the job market is today? Where have you been for the last few years?

Socrates: You wouldn't believe me if I told you. But we must ask just one more question, or rather two: What is a "good job" and why do you want one?

Peter: Money, of course. That's the answer to both questions. To all questions, maybe.

Socrates: I see. And what do you want to do with all the money you make?

Peter: You said your last two questions were your last.

Socrates: If you want to go away, I cannot keep you here. But if we pursue our explorations one little step further, we may discover something new.

Peter: What do you think you'll find? A new world?

Socrates: Quite possibly. A new world of thought. Will you come with me? Shall we trudge ahead through the swamps of our uncertainties? Or shall we sit comfortably at home in our little cave?

Peter: Why should I torture myself with all these silly questions from a strange little man? I'm supposed to be studying for my exam.

Socrates: Because it would be profitable for you. The unexamined life is not worth living, you know.

Peter: I heard that somewhere ... Good grief! That's one of the quotations that might be on my exam tomorrow. Who said that, anyway?

Socrates: I did. Didn't you hear me?

Peter: No, I mean who said it originally?

Socrates: It was I, I assure you. Now shall we continue our journey?

Peter: What are you getting at, anyway, Socrates?

Socrates: No, Peter, the question is what are *you* getting at? That is the topic we were exploring. Now shall we continue to make your life a little less unexamined and a little more worth living?

Peter: All right. For a little while, anyway.

Socrates: Then you will answer my last question?

Peter: I forgot what it was.

Socrates: What do you need money for?

Peter: Everything! Everything I want costs money.

Socrates: For instance?

Peter: Do you know how much it costs to raise a family nowadays?

Socrates: And what would you say is the largest expense in raising a family nowadays?

Peter: Probably sending the kids to college.

Socrates: I see. Let's review what you have said. You are reading this book to study for your exam, so that you can pass it and your course, to graduate and get a degree, to get a good job, to make a lot of money, to raise a family and send your children to college.

Peter: Right.

Socrates: And why will they go to college?

Peter: Same reason I'm here. To get good jobs, of course.

Socrates: So they can send their children to college?

Peter: Yes.

Socrates: Have you ever heard the expression "arguing in a circle"?

Peter: No, I never took logic.

Socrates: Really? I never would have guessed it.

Peter: You're teasing me.

Socrates: Really?

Peter: I'm a practical man. I don't care about logic, just life.

Socrates: Then perhaps we should call what you are doing "living in a circle." Have you ever asked yourself a terrifying, threatening question? What is the whole circle there for?

Peter: Hmmm ... nobody ever bothered me with that question before.

Socrates: I know. That is why I was sent to you.

Peter: Well, sending kids to college isn't the only thing I'm working for. I'm working for my own good to. That's not a circle, is it?

Socrates: We don't know until we look, do we? Tell me, what is "your own good"?

Peter: What do you mean?

Socrates: What benefit to yourself do you hope the money from a well-paying job will bring you?

Peter: All sorts of things. The good life. Fun and games. Leisure.

Socrates: I see. And you are now giving up fun and games for some serious studying so you can pass your exams and your courses and get your degree.

Peter: Right. It's called "delayed gratification." I could be watching the football game now, or playing poker. But I'm putting my time in the bank. It's an investment for the future. You see, when I'm set up in a good job, I'll be able to call my own shots.

Socrates: You mean you will then have leisure and be able to watch football games or play poker whenever you wish.

57

Peter: Right.

Socrates: Why don't you just do those things right now?

Peter: What?

Socrates: Why do you work instead of play if all you want to do is play? You're working now so that years from now you can have enough money to afford leisure to play. But you can play now. So why take the long, hard road if you're already home? It seems to be another circle back to where you started from, where you are now.

Peter: Are you telling me I should just drop out of school and goof off?

Socrates: No. I am telling you that you should find a good reason to be here. I don't think you have found that yet. Shall we keep searching?

Peter: All right, wise man or wise guy, whichever you are. You tell me. Why should I be here? What's the value of college? You've got a sermon up your sleeve, haven't you?

Socrates: Is that what you expect me to do?

Peter: Sure. Didn't you just tear down my answers so that you could sell me yours?

Socrates: Indeed not. I am not a wise man, only a philosopher, a lover and pursuer of wisdom, that divine but elusive goal.

Peter: What do you want with me then?

Socrates: To spread the infection of philosophizing.

Peter: So you're not going to teach me the answers?

Socrates: No. I think the most valuable lesson I could teach you is to become your own teacher. Isn't that one of the things you are here to learn? Isn't that one of the greatest values of a college education? Have none of your teachers taught you that? What has become of my great invention, anyway?

Peter: I guess I never looked at education that way.

Socrates: It's not too late to begin.

Peter: It is today, Socrates – or whoever you are. I'm really too busy today.

Socrates: Too busy to know why you're so busy? Too busy doing to know what you're doing?

Peter: Look, maybe we could continue this conversation some other time. I have more important things to do than this stuff.

Socrates: Philosophy. His stuff is philosophy. What exam are you studying for, by the way?

Peter: Well, actually, it's a philosophy exam.

Socrates: I see. I think you may be in trouble there.

Peter: No way. I've memorized the professors notes. I've got all the answers.

Socrates: And none of the questions. What is the value of your answers then?

Peter: I just can't waste my time on questions like that.

Socrates: Because you have to study philosophy?

Peter: Yes. Good-bye, strange little man.

Socrates: Good-bye, E.T. I hope some day you escape your circular wanderings and find your way home.

VI. Ten Philosophical Quotations that Are Relevant to Real Life

Reducing 2500 years of philosophy to ten relevant quotations would constitute an injustice to a long and storied tradition. The following quotations provide a sampling of the insight and guidance the *love of wisdom* offers.

1. *I say that man is condemned to be free. Condemned because he did not create himself, yet in other respects free; because once thrown into the world, he is responsible for everything he does* (Sartre, 1957, p. 23).

Although none of us entered the world with our consent, according to Jean-Paul Sartre eventually, after our arrival, we are responsible for the consequences of our actions. Outside of academia, where philosophers and psychologists perpetuate the *free will - determinism* debate, the reality of authentic choice-making is a given. The psychiatrist Irvin Yalom agrees with Sartre:

> Responsibility means authorship. To be aware of responsibility is to be aware of creating one's own self, destiny, life predicament, feelings, and, if such be the case, one's own suffering. For the patient who will not accept such responsibility, who persists in blaming others - either other individuals or other forces - for his

or her dysphoria (discontentment), no real therapy is possible (1980, p. 218).

2. *Hell is other people* (Sartre, 1948, p. 45).

This brief, well-known quotation speaks to interpersonal relationships. It comes from Sartre's play, *No Exit*, in which three characters arrive in hell to discover their fate is to spend a sleepless eternity together in a small room from which there is no escape. Each character is well suited to torment the other two. Predictably, eventually one of them declares, "Hell is other people." Although widely quoted this statement is often misunderstood as meaning human interactions and relationships are torturous. Sartre offers his intended meaning with this correction:

> "Hell is other people" has always been misunderstood. It has been thought that what I meant by that was that our relations with other people are always poisoned, that they are invariably hellish relations. But what I really mean is something totally different. I mean that if relations with someone else are twisted, vitiated, then that other person can only be hell. Why? Because when we think about ourselves, when we try to know ourselves … we use the knowledge of us which other people already have. We judge ourselves with the means other people have and have given us for judging ourselves. Into whatever I say about myself someone

else's judgment always enters. Into whatever I feel within myself someone else's judgment enters. But that does not mean at all that one cannot have relations with other people. It simply brings out the capital importance of all other people for each of us (2014).

3. *God is dead* (Neitzsche, 1974, p. 95).

Friedrich Nietzsche was an immoralist, which is not to say he was an evildoer. Rather, it means he challenged the established morality of his day. According to him we do not realize our own morality by blind conformity to a pre-existing code of conduct, like the Ten Commandments or Sermon on the Mount. Instead, our morality is declared by our actions. This credo is consistent with Nietzsche's atheism, which he addressed in his last book, *Ecce Homo: How One Becomes What One Is,* completed shortly before he descended into the insanity that lasted until his death. There he writes, "I have absolutely no knowledge of atheism as an outcome of reasoning, still less as an event; with me it is obviously by instinct" (2014).

His bold, infamous declaration, "God is dead," is more a sociological statement than a theological assertion (1974, p. 95). Nietzsche did not believe in a literal God who once lived and then died. Rather, he believed the failure of human beings to live as though they believed in God rendered religious faith meaningless and God functionally dead.

"Whither is God?" he (the madman) cried, "I shall tell you. We have killed him - you and I. All of us are his murderers ... God is dead ... And we have killed him. How shall we, the murderers of all murderers, comfort ourselves?" (p. 95).

For Nietzsche, "the end of Christianity (meant) the advent of nihilism" (Craig, 2008, p. 77). For centuries humankind had depended on God for a moral code to effect social order. Without God there is no authority for a code of conduct binding upon all human beings. A statement attributed to Fyodor Dostoevsky describes this situation: "If God does not exist then all things are possible" (2014). Nietzsche posited if God or some other absolute moral authority does not exist then we are left with moral anarchy. Nevertheless, he saw something redemptive emerging from this moral chaos: each of us bears responsibility for constructing and living out a self-determined morality.

Like Freud, Nietzsche believed the time had come to move beyond belief in God and the practice of religion. In *The Gay Science* he writes, "Belief in the Christian God has become unbelievable." (1974, p. 343). An existentialist, he taught it is our actions that define us, not our words. Accordingly, he writes: "Of all that is written, I love only what a person hath written with his blood" (2019).

4. *That which does not kill me makes me stronger* (Nietzsche, 1997, p. 6).

Intended as a word of encouragement, this thought from Nietzsche is often quoted by a speaker who is unaware of its source. It is similar to the concept of *tragic optimism*, Frankl's belief that we can use life's three inevitable tragedies (pain, guilt, and death) to make us stronger and better people.

5. *The unexamined life is not worth living* (Plato, 1914, 38a.5-6).

These words, recorded by Plato in *The Apology of Socrates*, express Socrates' belief that an excellent life is one in which we understand why we think, feel, and act as we do. This self-understanding requires a commitment to introspection, which makes this quotation seem an encouragement to engage in psychotherapy. (Note: This quotation also appears in chapter III.)

6. *Happiness proves to be activity of the soul in accord with virtue* (1999, 109a.15).

This is Aristotle's formula for a flourishing life. (Although the Greek *eudaimonia* is often translated as "happiness," its more precise meaning is "flourishing.") According to Aristotle, a well-lived life consists of meaningful activity and adherence to an internalized moral code. (Note: This quotation also appears in chapter III.)

7. *You will never be happy if you continue to search for what happiness consists of. You will never live if you are looking for the meaning of life* (Camus, 2019).

Camus understood happiness is like sawdust. Just as sawdust is the by-product of the activity of sawing wood, so also happiness is the derivative of meaningful activity (as Aristotle believed). Camus' existential response to the unanswerable question of life's meaning is similar to and consistent with an assessment made by Frankl: "What matters, therefore, is not the meaning of life in general but rather the specific meaning of a person's life at a given moment" (1959, p. 131). Camus and Frankl believed the meaning of life is constructed by actions rather than discovered through contemplation. (Note: This quotation also appears in chapter III.)

8. *I recommend that the Statue of Liberty on the East Coast be supplemented by a Statue of Responsibility on the West Coast* (Frankl, 1959, p. 156).

Responsibility is an important word in the vocabulary of existentialists. Frankl considered responsibility so important he suggested a Statue of Responsibility as a counterbalance to the Statue of Liberty. Notwithstanding, a man does not have to be an existentialist to acknowledge with freedom comes responsibility. (Note: This quotation also appears in chapter I.)

9. *A man can do what he wills but he cannot will what he wills* (Schopenhauer, 1973, p. 6).

"You cannot keep birds from flying over your head but you can keep them from building a nest in your hair" (2019). Martin Luther used this metaphor to express his belief that we are responsible only for those thoughts that we turn into actions. Arthur Schopenhauer, a 19th century German philosopher, also believed our moral status is determined by what we do rather than what we imagine. In fact, when we restrain ourselves from acting on an immoral thought we demonstrate admirable character. Schopenhauer's words are clarified by this paraphrase: *A man can do what he desires, but he cannot choose what to desire.*

10. *The real question of life after death isn't whether or not it exists, but even if it does what problem this really solves* (Wittgenstein, 2019).

Ludwig Wittgenstein insisted philosophers should pursue answers to practical questions. Unless the thought of eternal reward for a moral life or eternal punishment for an immoral life influences our conduct then the afterlife question is meaningless. An implication of Wittgenstein's assertion is even for those who believe in an afterlife this belief has little or no influence on their pre-death conduct.

Glossary

Absolute Truth (Absolutism) A belief that is unaffected by circumstances is a belief that is held *absolutely*. To believe something *absolutely* is to believe it unconditionally; that there are no circumstances that will alter the belief.

Abstract The characteristic of being conceptual rather than physical.

Abstruse The characteristic of being profound and difficult to understand.

Aesthetics It is the subcategory of philosophy concerned with understanding the experience of beauty and pleasure. It addresses the question of why certain things are pleasing to the senses.

Anecdotal Data Information resulting from experiences rather than formal research. Such information can be a single case or collection of several cases.

Argument A presentation that supports a point-of-view; a case for accepting something as true.

Argumentum ad Baculum (Argument of Force) A logical fallacy in which fear or intimidation is used to support an idea.

Max Malikow

Argumentum ad Ignorantium (Argument of Ignorance) A logical fallacy in which an absence of proof of something is erroneously concluded as proof of its absence.

Argumentum ad Vercundiam (Argument of Authority) A logical fallacy in which an expert in one field provides an opinion that is irrelevant because the topic under consideration is outside of the expert's field.

Aristotle's Principle of the Golden Mean Aristotle characterized a virtue as the apex (i.e. high-point) between two vices. For example, courage is the virtue located between the two vices of recklessness and cowardice.

Cause-and-Effect A relationship in which event-A precedes event-B and it can be demonstrated that event-A is the reason why event-B occurred.

Cogito ergo sum. ("I think, therefore, I am.") One of philosophy's best-known quotations, these are the words of Rene Descartes. He concluded that his existence was the one thing of which he could be certain. Even if every other thought he had was incorrect, the fact that he was thinking proved his existence.

Correlation A relationship between two events tending to occur together, calling for further investigation of the relationship.

70

Cost-Benefit Analysis The practice in business and industry of comparing the expense of two or more courses of action to help decide which one to take.

Cosmological Argument One of the so-called *rational proofs for the existence of God* by which it is reasoned that the universe could not have created itself. In this argument God is referred to as the *universe-maker*.

Deductive Reasoning The logical process by which a conclusion necessarily follows from principles; thinking from general to specific. For example, it might be concluded that Abraham Lincoln was a great President if criteria for "presidential greatness" (general) are established and Lincoln (specific) meets the criteria.

Deontological Ethics The determination of moral behavior based upon a duty to obey certain rules of conduct. The Ten Commandments is an example of a deontological code of conduct. The term deontological is derived from the Greek word for "duty" (*deon*).

Dualism The belief that reality consists of two fundamentally different entities: the physical and the nonphysical. Dualism is related to the *mind-body problem*.

Empirical The characteristic of demonstration to show that something is true. Scientific experiments are commonly referred to as empirical proof.

Endurance In aesthetic philosophy, this is one of the three criteria by which a work of art, literature or music is evaluated as a classic. *Endurance* refers to a work having passed the test of time. The other two criteria are *universality* and *recognition*.

Epistemology The subcategory of philosophy concerned with knowledge. Specifically, it is concerned with how knowledge is acquired and the means by which certainty of knowledge is achieved.

Ethics The subcategory of philosophy concerned with right moral conduct.

Ethnological Argument One of the so-called *rational proofs for the existence of God*, it is based on the belief that all races and cultures of human beings throughout history have practiced religion. This curiosity about the supernatural and a Supreme Being is the result of God having made people in such a way as to investigate a religious life.

Fallacy This is the general term for any error in logic; a flaw in reasoning.

Fallacy of Causal Connection A logical fallacy in which one event or condition is erroneously believed to be the explanation for another event or condition. This implies that the correct explanation has been overlooked.

Free Will In philosophy, this is understood as the ability to make authentic choices; to act in accordance with one's strongest motive. It is widely believed that free will makes human beings responsible for their behavior.

God In monotheistic (one-god) religions, God is the Supreme Being with the qualities of omniscience (all-knowing), omnipotence (all-powerful), ubiquitous (present everywhere), and pre-existence (prior to the universe).

Happiness In both philosophy and psychology this is understood as overall contentment with one's life.

Historical Proof One of the three categories of truth, it is knowledge of the past based on testimony.

Intervening Variable Related to the fallacy of causal connection, it is the overlooked event or condition that is the correct explanation for the event or condition under investigation. For example, the correct explanation for the high rate of suicide among police officers is not the nature of their work but the immediate availability of a firearm.

Inductive Reasoning This is a logical process that progresses from specific to general. For example, the criteria for "great Presidents" would be *deduced* from first making a list of great Presidents and then evaluating what they had in common.

Law of Non-Contradiction This is the rule of logic that a statement cannot be true if it speaks against itself. For example, the statement, "There is no truth" negates itself, because if *there is no truth* it would include the statement itself.

Logic The subcategory of philosophy that is concerned with correct reasoning.

Metaphysics The subcategory of philosophy that is concerned with reality outside of the physical realm; it addresses questions that cannot be investigated scientifically or historically. Examples of metaphysical questions are: *How did the universe come into existence? Does God exist? Is there an afterlife? What is the meaning of life?*

Mind-Body Problem If human beings have a nonphysical entity that directs the mental processes (i.e. the mind), how does that which is nonphysical contact and influence that which is physical (i.e. the body)?

Moral Argument One of the so-called *rational proofs for the existence of God* by which it is reasoned that if justice is to have any meaning there must be an ultimate Judge (God). Injustice often prevails in the world. Nevertheless, the longing for justice is so great that it must be more than a mere concept, implying a judge (God) who is able to administer justice outside of human history.

Ontological Argument Perhaps the weakest of the *so-called rational proofs for the existence of God* in which God is defined as the greatest Being imaginable. As such, God has all good qualities to the infinite degree. Since actual existence is better than imaginary existence, God must have actual existence. Therefore, God exists.

Ought This is a one-word summary of ethical philosophy, referring to how people *should* behave.

Overgeneralization The logical fallacy of saying too much from too little data. A common instance of this fallacy is assuming a principle from a single case or event.

Philosophical Proof The test for truth used by philosophers in contrast to the methods employed by historians and scientists. Historical truth is established by way of evidence and testimony. Scientific truth is demonstrated by experimentation. A philosopher tests a statement for truth by asking three questions: (1) Does this statement contradict itself? (2) Does this statement correspond to reality as demonstrated by science and experienced by most people? (3)

Is this statement of practical use? Although a philosopher's methodology cannot always verify a statement, it can often falsify a statement.

Philosophy Defined as the love and pursuit of wisdom by intellectual means; *philosophy* is derived from the Greek words for love (*philein*) and knowledge (*sophos*).

Plato's Allegory of the Cave This is Plato's representation of human beings as chained in place by their culture, education, and experience and therefore unable to attain complete knowledge. Plato believed that individuals, at best, can have a perspective on the truth of a subject.

Plato's Concept of the Mind Plato conceptualized the mind (the entity that directs the mental processes) as consisting of *appetites* (feelings), *reason* (intellect), and the *spirited element* (the person each of us would like to be). He reasoned that when feelings and intellect were in conflict, the spirited element would influence the person to act honorably.

Primer A textbook that explains the basic principles of a subject.

Psychology The science of mind and behavior that attempts to explain why people think, act, and feel as they do. An alternative definition is *the study of human behavior.*

Plausible Rival Hypothesis An alternative explanation that is compatible with the facts of an event and therefore acceptable.

Rational Proofs for God's Existence The five arguments that favor the existence of God: *cosmological, ethnological, moral, ontological,* and *teleological.* Although referred to as "proofs," they are attempts to make an intellectual case for the existence of God.

Recognition A term used in aesthetic philosophy that refers to experts' opinion that a work of art is a classic. *Endurance* and *universality* are two other criteria used in evaluating a work as a classic.

Relative Truth (Relativism) In contrast to *absolutism,* relativism refers to something that is true under certain conditions. For example, when someone speaks of something as absolutely true it means that there are no conditions that will make it untrue. If something is relatively true it means that it is true only under certain conditions.

Religion Although frequently defined as a system of worship expressing belief in a god or gods, an alternative definition is *intensive and comprehensive belief.*

Scientific Proof The methodology for establishing something as true by way of the four-step procedure of observation, hypothesis, experimentation, and conclusion. This type of proof is also referred to as *empirical demonstration.*

Skeptic One who habitually doubts; historically, a follower of the Greek philosopher Pyrrho of Elis.

Syllogism A form of deductive reasoning used in logic and consisting of a major premise, minor premise, and conclusion. A common illustration of a syllogism is: All men are mortal (major premise) ... Socrates is a man (minor premise) ... Therefore, Socrates is mortal (conclusion).

Teleological Argument One of the five so-called *rational proofs for the existence of God* in which it is stated that order and predictability in the universe imply that the universe is not the product of random events but an intelligent design. The *intelligent designer* is God.

Teleological Ethics In contrast to *deontological ethics,* teleological ethical systems determine moral right by the achievement of a desired goal. Teleological is derived from the Greek word for "end" (*telos*). Teleological ethics can be characterized by the phrase "the end justifies the means."

Universality A term from aesthetic philosophy and one of the three criteria for evaluating a work of art as a classic. If an artistic work has appeal among a diversity of cultures then it is said to have universality. *Endurance* and *recognition* are the other two criteria.

Value Theory The subcategory of philosophy concerned with the evaluation of the worth of something. It is often applied in decision-making when the relative worth of two things are part of a decision-making process.

References

Introduction

Jobs, S. (2014). Recovered from the 06/15/2005 news.stanford.-edu/news website on 07/04/2014.

Chapter I

Browne, K. (2011). *Philosophical observations*. Charleston, SC: CreateSpace Publishing.

_____. (2019). Recovered from http://kevinjbrowne. weekly.com/articles.html on 07/31/2019.

Burroughs, A. (2012). *This is how: Surviving what you think you can't.* New York: Picador.

Epictetus. Recovered from https://www.brainyquote.com /quotes/epictetus_105597 on 07/26/2019.

Frankl, V. (1992). *Man's search for meaning*. Boston: Beacon Press.

_____. (1959). *Man's search for meaning*. New York: Washington Square Press.

Harris, S. (2019). Recovered from https://c13. Google usercontent.com/ on 07/26/2019.

James, W. (1907). "The Present Dilemma in Philosophy". Lecture I in Pragmatism: A new name for some old ways of thinking. New York: Longman Green and Co.

Luther, M. (2019). Recovered from https://www.goodreads. com/.../757798-you-cannot-keep-birds-from-flying-over-your on 07/31/2019.

Malikow, M. (2011). *Philosophy reader: Essays and articles for thought and discussion.* Charlestown, SC: CreateSpace Independent Publishing Platform.

Milton, J. (1667). *Paradise lost.* London, UK: Samuel Simmons.

Philosophers playing soccer." (1972). "Monty python's fliegender zirkus. Broadcast 12/18/1972.

Rousseau, J. (1968). *Social contract.* New York: Penguin Classics.

Sartre, J. (1957). *Existentialism and human emotions.* New York: Kensington Publishing Group.

Spence, G. (1996). *How to argue and win every time: At home, at work, in court, everywhere, every day.* New York: St. Martin's Press.

Wittgenstin, L. (2009). *Philosophical investigations*, Revised 4th edition.translated by G.E.M. Anscombe, P.M.S. Hacker, and Joachim Schulte. Hoboken, NJ: Wiley-Blackwell.

Chapter II

Camus, A. (1955). *The myth of Sisyphus and other essays.* New York: Alfred A. Knopf, Inc.

Carnegie, A. (1889). "Wealth." North American review. June, 1889.

Klagge, J. (2016). *Simply Wittgenstein*. New York: Simply Charly.

Marx, K. (1998). *The German ideology: Including theses on Feuerbach*. New York: Prometheus Books.

Rand, A. (1961). *The virtue of selfishness*. New York: Penguin Books.

Robinson, D. (2004). *The great ideas of philosophy, 2nd edition*. Lecture 2: "Did the Greeks invent philosophy?" Chantilly, VA: The Teaching Company.

Weaver, R. (1948). *Ideas have consequences*. Chicago, IL: The University of Chicago Press.

Wittgenstin, L. (2009). *Philosophical investigations*, Revised 4th edition translated by G.E.M. Anscombe, P.M.S. Hacker, and Joachim Schulte. Hoboken, NJ: Wiley-Blackwell.

Chapter III

Aristotle (1999). *Nichomachean ethics*. second edition. T. Irwin, translator. Indianapolis, IN: Hackett Publishing Company.

_____ (2009). *Nichomachean ethics*. Leslie Brown, (editor). David Rose (translator). Oxford, UK: Oxford University Press.

Benet, S. (1942). "A Child Is Born." *We Stand United and Other Radio Scripts*. New York: Rinehart and Co.

Camus, A. (2019). Recovered from https://stoicanswers .com/2018/03/06no-questions-please-albert-camus on 09/01/2019.

Epicurus (2015). "Letter to Menoeceus." Recovered from www.epicurus.net website April 2015.

Garfield, J. (2013). *The meaning of life: Perspectives from the world's great intellectual traditions*. Chantilly, VA: The Teaching Company.

Gray, T. (1889). "Ode to a distant prospect of Eton college." *The selected poems of Thomas Gray*. New York: White. Stokes, and Allen.

Hawthorne, N. (1978). *The scarlet letter*. New York: W.W. Norton.

Hoffer, E. (1983). *Truth imagined*. New York: Harper & Row Publishers.

Johnson, L. (2007). "Practical philosophy: The greco-roman moralists." Chantilly, VA: The Teaching Company.

Jung, C. (1933). *Modern man in search of a soul*. New York: Little, Brown, and Company.

King, M. (1968). "I've been to the mountaintop speech." Given in Memphis, TN on 04/03/1968.

Klagge, J. (2016). *Simply Wittgenstein*. New York: Simply Charly.

Mill, J. (2001). *Utilitarianism.* Indianapolis, IN: Hackett Publishing Company.

Plato (1914). *Euthyphro, Apology, Crito, Phaedo, Phaedrus.* Harold N. Fowler, translator. Cambridge, MA: Loeb Classical Library. Harvard University Press.

Publishers Weekly. (2006). Recovered from http://www.amazon.com/gp/product on 06/19/2006.

Robinson, D. (2004). *The great ideas of philosophy,* 2nd edition. Lecture #50: "Four Theories of a Good Life." Chantilly, VA: The Teaching Company.

Rokeach, M. (1964). *The three christs of Ypsilanti.* New York: Vintage Books.

Socrates (2019). Recovered from https://www.goodreads.com/quotes/73059-i-cannot-teach-anybody-anything-i-can-only-make-them on 09/04/2019.

Trueblood, D. (1951). *The Life We Prize.* New York: Harper and Brothers.

Waller, R. (1992). *The bridges of Madison county.* New York: Warner Books.

Chapter IV

Descartes, R. (2019). Recovered from Oxford University Press. *Oxford dictionaries* lexico.com/definitions /cogito on 12/22/2019.

Kilpatrick, W. (1992). *Why Johnny can't tell right from wrong. Moral illiteracy and the case for character education.*New York: Simon & Schuster.

Malikow, M. (2010). *Being human: Philosophical reflections on psychological issues.* Lanham, MD: Hamilton Books.

Nagel, T. (1986). *The view from nowhere.* New York: Oxford University Press.

_____. (1974). "What is it like to be a bat?" *The philosophical review.* 83 (4). 435-450.

Nietzsche, F. (1976). *Thus spake Zarathustra: A book for all or none.* Walter Kaufmann, translator. New York: Random House.

Yalom, I. (2008). *Staring at the sun. Overcoming the terror of death.* San Franciso, CA: Jossey Bass.

Chapter V

Kreeft, P. (1984). *The best things in life: A 20th century Socrates looks at power, pleasure, truth, and the good life.* Downers Grove, IL: Inter Varsity Press.

Chapter VI

Aristotle (1999). *Nichomachean ethics.* second edition. T. Irwin, translator. Indianapolis, IN: Hackett Publishing Company.

Camus, A. (2019). Recovered from https://stoicanswers
.com/2018/03/06no-questions-please-albert-camus on
09/01/2019.

Craig, W. (2008). *Reasonable faith: Christian theology and apologetics*. Wheaton, IL: Crossway Books.

Dostoevsky, F. (2014). Although this quotation has frequently been attributed to Fyodor Dostoevsky as part of *The Brothers Karamazov* it is nowhere to be found in this work. However, the idea conveyed by this quotation is present in the book. The closest quotation in the book is: "If there is no immortality, then all things are permitted" (Dostoevsky, F. *The brothers Karamazov*. translated C. Garnett. New York: Signet Classics. 1957. book II, chapter 6; book V, chapter 4; book XI, chapter 8.

Frankl, V. (1959). *Man's search for meaning*. New York: Washington Square Press.

Luther, M. (2019). Recovered from https://www/goodreads. com >quotes>757798-you-cannot-keep-birds-from-flying on 12/30/2019.

Martin. (1989). *Ethics* (Translated: J.A.K. Thompson and H. Tredennick, NY: Penguin). Recovered from Martin, M. 1989. p. 40. *Everyday morality: An introduction to applied ethics*. Belmont, CA: Wadsworth Publishing.

Nietzsche, F. (1997). *Twilight of the idols*. Indianapolis, IN: Hackett Publishing Company.

Nietzsche, F. (2019). Recovered from> friedrich_nietzsche _101616 on 12/29/2019.

_____ . (1974). *The gay science*. Walter Kaufmann, translator. New York: Vintage Books.

Plato (1914). *Euthyphro, Apology, Crito, Phaedo, Phaedrus*. Harold N. Fowler, translator. Cambridge, MA: Loeb Classical Library. Harvard University Press.

Sartre, J. (1957). *Existentialism and human emotions*. New York: Kensington Publishing Group.

_____ . (1948). *No exit*. New York: Alfred A. Knopf.

_____ . (2014). Recovered from Ambrosino, B. "Hell is other people misquoting philosophers." Recovered from brandon@vox.com on 10/13/2019.

Schopenhauer, A. (1973). *Essays and aphorisms*. New York: Penguin Classics.

Wittgenstein, L. (2019). Recovered from https://www. goodreads.com /quotes/69091-the-real-question-of-life-after-death-isnt-whether-or on 12/30/2019.

Yalom, I. (1980). *Existential psychotherapy*. New York: Basic Books, Inc. Publishers.

About the Author

Max Malikow has taught philosophy for over 30 years. He holds a master's degree from Gordon-Conwell Theological Seminary and doctorate from Boston University. Currently, he is on the faculty of the Renee Crown Honors Program of Syracuse University and an Adjunct Assistant Professor of Philosophy at LeMoyne College. He is the author of 17 other books and a practicing psychotherapist in Syracuse, New York.

Other Books by Max Malikow

Why is Life So Difficult? Reflections and Suggestions.

Six Paths to a Good Life

Heroism and Virtue: Reflections on Human Greatness

Buried Above Ground: Understanding Suicide and the Suicidal Mind

Christ the Counselor: Reflecting on Jesus as a Therapist.

It Happened in Little Valley: A Case Study of Uxoricide

Death: Reflections on the End of Life and What Comes After.

Mere Existentialism: A Primer

It's Not Too Late! Making the Most of the Rest of Your Life (third edition)

The Human Predicament: Towards an Understanding of the Human Situation

Philosophy Reader: Essays and Articles for Thought and Discussion

Being Human: Philosophical Reflections on Psychological Issues

Philosophy 101: A Primer for the Apathetic or Struggling Student

Suicidal Thoughts: Essays on Self-Determined Death

Profiles in Character: Twenty-Six Stories that Will Instruct and Inspire Teenagers

Teachers for Life: Advice and Methods Gathered Along the Way

Living When a Young Friend Commits Suicide: Or Is Even Thinking About It (co-authored with Rabbi Dr. Earl A. Grollman)